ALL AMERICAN POET

WENDELL PATRICK CARTER

I0558935

CURRY BROTHERS PUBLISHING

ISBN: 979-8-9907516-8-2

Request for information should be addressed to: Curry Brothers Marketing and Publishing Group

P.O. Box 247 Haymarket, VA 20168

Cover Design: Vibranium Media Group
Executive Editing: Gerald D. Curry

ALL AMERICAN POET

WENDELL PATRICK CARTER

CURRY BROTHERS PUBLISHING

CONTENTS

DEDICATION

To Coach Bowden and all my teammates for without them these poems
could not exist.

INTRODUCTION

My name is Wendell Patrick Carter and I played for the Seminoles from 1984-1987. I came to FSU highly recruited out of Sarasota Riverview High School. During a time when Coach Bowden was building something special in Tallahassee. These poems were created to introduce a new generation of Seminole fans to some of the great players, events and history surrounding the FSU program during that time frame.

Guys like Mark Salva, Jason Kuipers and Joey Ionata to name a few, are some of the building blocks of the FSU program that helped Coach Bowden begin his unprecedented 15 year run.

From 1987 to 2000, the Seminoles finished every season with at least 10 wins and in the top 5 of the Associated Press College Football Poll, and won the national championship in 1993 and 1999.

My junior year 1986, I was Honorable Mention All-American and my senior season culminated with me being named 2nd All-American.

I was later drafted by the Detroit Lions and played in the National Football League for 10 seasons. I also later coached 5 more seasons with the St. Louis Rams and Detroit Lions.

Today I write poetry and I hope this helps comprehend the title of the my book, All-American Poet.

CLASS OF
EIGHTY-FO

ONE THING ABOUT THE FSU CLASS OF
EIGHTY-FO
WE WERE A BUNCH OF NO-NAMES THAT
HELPED THE PROGRAM GROW
CLASS OF 85 GETS ALL THE SHINE
OUR CREW WERE THE ONES THAT DID THE
GRIND
WE HAD 4 STARTERS, UP ON THE FRONT
MCGOWAN AND SHIVE, LOVED TO HUNT
FELTON, GABBARD AND PALMER ALSO RAN
STUNTS
DEREK SCHMIDT WAS THE KICKER THAT
COULD ALSO PUNT
MCDUFFIE AND ANDREWS WERE ALWAYS
BLUNT
THEY HAD TO BE PLEASED, A BUNCH OF US
STARTED
THIS WAS A WHOLE NEW PROGRAM AS WE
DEPARTED

By Wendell Patrick Carter

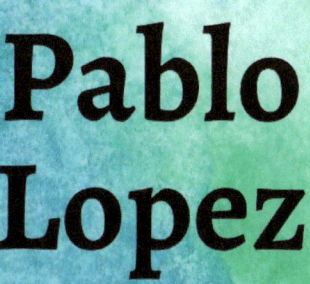

Pablo Lopez

I know it was September of 1986
An instant, time has not fully fixed
We were together that day
All of a sudden you were gone away
Pastor Ken announced your death
That moment I lost my breath
But God doesn't make mistakes
But for your family my heart still aches.

By Wendell Patrick Carter

HE PLAYED WITH ME

By Wendell Patrick Carter

WHEN IT'S DISCOVERED THAT I PLAYED IN TALLAHASSEE
I'M OFTEN ASKED, DID YOU PLAY WITH THAT DUDE THAT'S FLASHY
I ALWAYS SAY, HE AND I ARE REAL COOL
BUT I WAS A STARTER, WHEN HE'S IN HIGH SCHOOL
THERE WAS NO DENYING HIS SHINE
NOT BAD TO ASSUME, I PLAYED WITH PRIME
BUT OVER ON OFFENSE, I'M GETTING MINE
DOMINATING, WHIPPING TREMENDOUS BEHIND
MY CLASS ARRIVED A YEAR BEFORE HIS CREW
AND WITH THEIR ADDITIONS OUR STRENGTH GREW
IF YOU FOLLOWED ALONG, IT WAS PLAIN TO SEE, THAT COACH PRIME, PLAYED WITH ME.

MATT drills

Matt Drills was our college off season
conditioning
When they recruit you, they were careful to
never mentioning
It's one of the most difficult things I've had to
endure
But when it's over your body is so pure
The toxins were removed for sure
It teaches you to push your body to the
extreme
During games, you're not tired as you seem
In the NFL I used as a reminder when I felt I
was tired
It worked pretty well And it kept me hired

THE BIG III

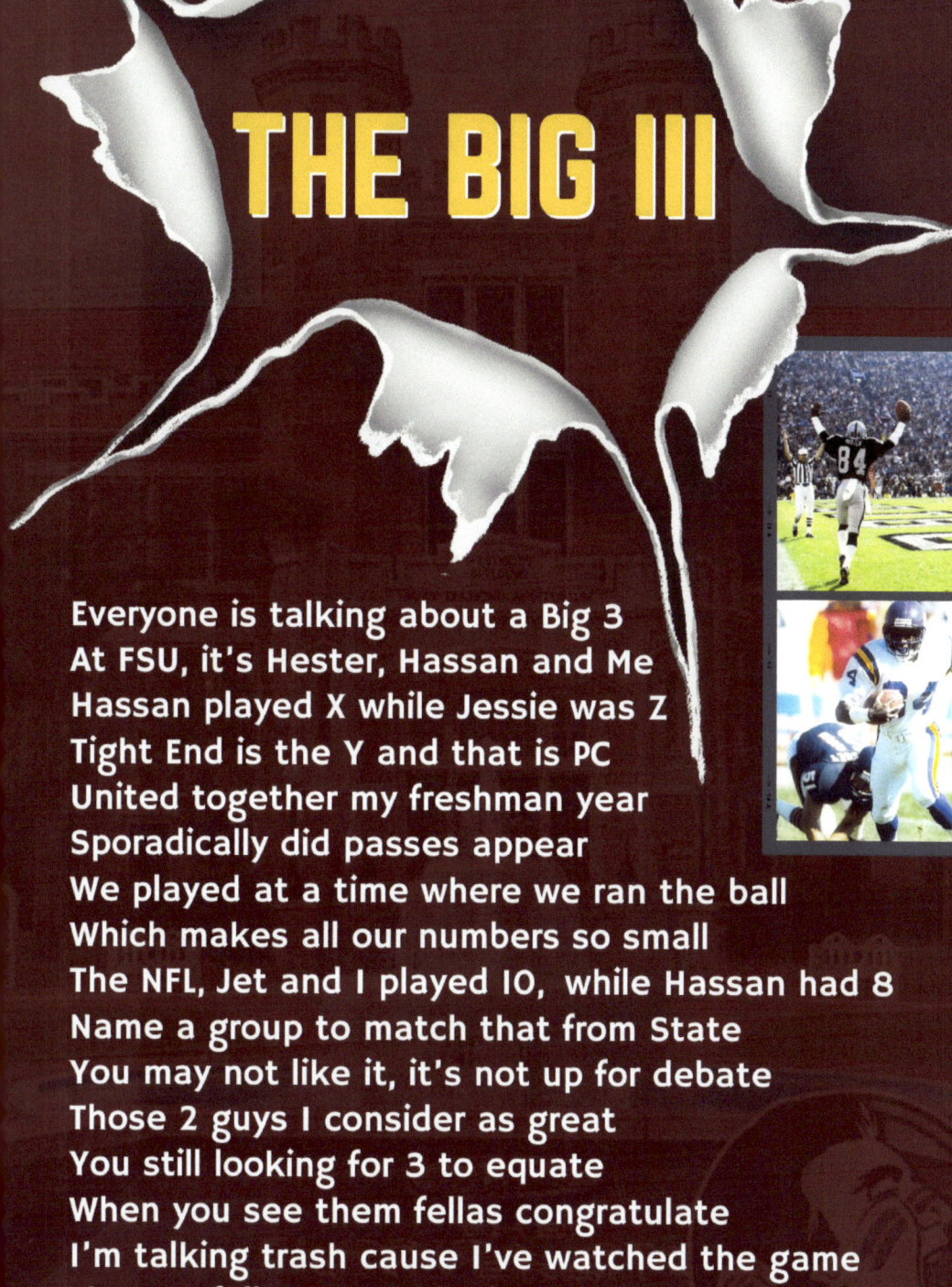

Everyone is talking about a Big 3
At FSU, it's Hester, Hassan and Me
Hassan played X while Jessie was Z
Tight End is the Y and that is PC
United together my freshman year
Sporadically did passes appear
We played at a time where we ran the ball
Which makes all our numbers so small
The NFL, Jet and I played 10, while Hassan had 8
Name a group to match that from State
You may not like it, it's not up for debate
Those 2 guys I consider as great
You still looking for 3 to equate
When you see them fellas congratulate
I'm talking trash cause I've watched the game
Those 2 fellas should be in FSU's Hall of Fame.

COBLE
TERRACE

Coble Terrace was the name of our dorm
Only football players, was the norm
Tracey Sanders was my roommate
Hung with E and Herb, where I got a plate
Cletis had the Mustang that squeeked
Someone at the pool streaked
Played chess with Billy Allen and Chavers
Billy had a closet full of tank tops all flavors
Fred and Pablo was where I saw Scarface
Played Atari some mornings at Deion's place
Thala and Randy was where we gambled
Jesse Soloman was known to ramble
While, Bruce Heggie he had a snake
Stiehl and Barco their necks they almost break
Planning the Great Window Escape
I love that place good times there
Those that know only we share

PHI BETA SIGMA

Phi Beta Sigma is my fraternity
Sorry bros, I'm delinquent currently
Met some really good brothers all over these lands

Eric, Herb and Gaylon are my sands
Mighty Mu Epsilon is our chapter home
And Alpha Eta brothers also roamed
A lot of NFL brothers I also knew

Emmitt, Lomas and James Washington are a few
People accuse me of being an enigma
No ma'am I am just a mighty Sigma.

#85

I had this number back in 10th grade
Coach Lloyd Daugherty, decision was made
At FSU, from David Ponder after he played
The number was back on the offensive side
And you better believe I wore it with pride
Wore it all 4 years I was the starter
You say 85, yeah that's Pat Carter
Folks I notice have a short memory
Those who wore it after, were supposed to be
the next me
Thank God he only made one
Jewell and Maggie's grandson
On the football field is where I thrived
Proudly wearing the number 85

WHAT YOU DOING HERE?

That was the question that was asked to me
I told her I'm in this class, to get a college degree
This was college math 1141
This class was tough, not much fun
When she asked, she said really it strong
Eyed me, and scowled, as if I I didn't belong
Her big problem, if I can recall
Is only because I played football
She assumed that we were all dumb
But that really showed her intelligence was numb
After finals, she HAD to be appalled
When she saw my higher grade on the wall.

$$S = \frac{a \times b}{2}$$

The Phyrst was a pub near the school
A place in Tallahassee I considered cool
The first place I ate Buffalo wings
But Bladder Bust was their big thing
Free beer until one leaves out
There players prevented any move about
Once our table was full of beer
We made sure the coast was clear
A great place to bond with our peers
I enjoyed that place for a couple of years.

SAMMIE SMITH

I am really proud of this guy
When we err young, thank God we don't die
Admire those that recover after a fall
Dust themselves off, standing tall
He did his time, paid the price
A free man now, seeking his slice
Got rid of any bad vice
Commissioned, to bring others to Christ
And also giving sound advice
He's done it now, for me twice
On a mission to help many others
An excellent speaker I also discovered
God has given him the Victory
And I'll always support his ministry.

Scan to support Sammie Smith

FOOTBALL HUMBLES

No matter how great a player you are
Football will humble you, Free Agent or Star
It's the divine nature of this sport
It's just the way the game sorts
It reminds you to stay humble
Cause you can quickly tumble
Never be overconfident
It's disrespect to your opponent
You've seen star players lose the game
And the coach will take all the blame
But you better believe that player is shame
Fans calling him out of his name
That's just how the cookie crumbles
Football Humbles.

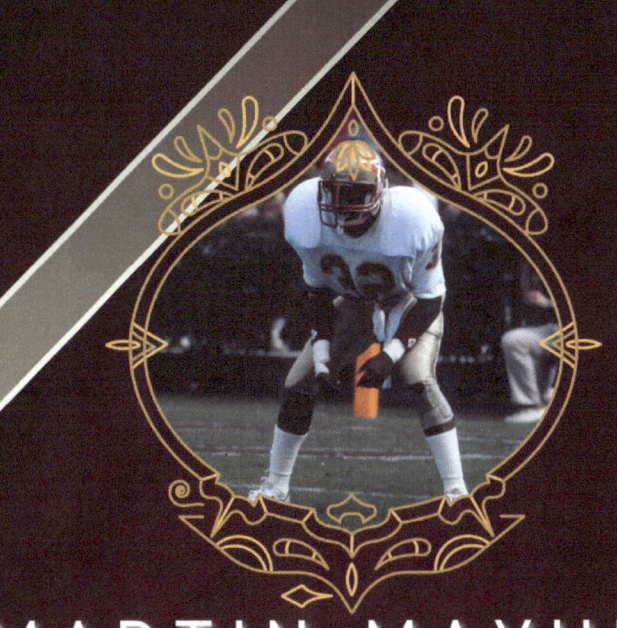

MARTIN MAYHEW

Freshman year I just couldn't resist
It was picture day, saw a beautiful miss
It was Mayhew's girl, didn't know this
He saw me staring and got pissed
I was wrong about that, I must say
I've always admired him, since that day
It wasn't because of his reaction
His smarts grabbed my attraction
An excellent student and playmaker on the field
Hadn't met a guy that produced that kinda yield
Later worked together in Motown
Unfortunately our results left us with frowns
Even today if he comes to town
We'll eat lunch and have a rundown
I'm not surprised by the heights he attained
He's a real good brother whose dreams weren't
restrained

AUBURN GAME
AUBURN SENIOR YEAR

Auburn game, my senior year
On the side of my helmet, was the Spear
Jordan-Hare Stadium, came to make clear
It's the FSU Seminoles, you better fear
Fans in the bleachers, drinking beer
Between sips, continued to jeer
Coach turned me loose, it was my premier
Stadium became silent, as we began to smear
They couldn't cover us, DBs interfered
How bad you beat them, pretty severe
Sports Illustrated Cover, lost to my peer
Derek Schmidt ended, all-time scorer in his
career.

SHIVE

There was a guy in college that could make
dudes squeal
I had to know where he was on the practice field
I was pretty smart, at least far from dumb
Just wanted to know from where that heat would
come
Caught a pass, he hit me in the ear
For a moment I couldn't think clear
Coach Andrews was a really great molder
Shive hit a guy who dislocated both shoulders
He hit guys that needed to be carried away
This man really hunted for prey
Thank goodness I was bigger in weight
Or I'd have lost a lot to my classmate

SKiMAsK

There's an incident I can clearly recollect
It happened at FSU after bed check
Assistant coaches assigned with the task
I look out the window, 2 dudes fleeing in
ski masks
That was found with so much humor
It was Pat White and Dodge was the rumor
The gossip soon died down
There's only 1 person 6'3" 160lbs
So, as I watch their attempt to dislodge
I was confident it was Dedrick Dodge

MRS. BETTY'S

Mrs. Betty's we called our training table
The food was good, I'm telling no fable
We had to check in at daybreak
Their way of making sure we were awake
While there, I definitely got a plate
The real cause of me gaining weight
Had a dude who stayed bothering me
We cracked jokes on each other,
John Hadley Pasco's fried chicken was the rave
That steak and fried shrimp were also craved
John Eaford held court in that place
He stayed on Fred Jones gave no grace
Many wild stories there were told
Anything you wanted to drink, hot or cold
Fellas snuck food back to the room
Had a full belly ready for the Moon
Good food, good laughs I'll always treasure
Thankful that I had that pleasure.

YOUNG PUPS

My senior year we needed youngsters to step up
They could no longer hide being a pup
Ronald, Edgar and Dex answered the call
But Haywood Haynes stomped hardest of all
He thought I was hard on him
I was sure he was ready to step out on a limb

We'd not have been as good without these guys
They are part of the reason of the schools rise
Ended that season with 11 wins
Ronald says 12 if we throw the deep end.

FSU
FLORIDA STATE
U N I V E R S I T Y

ACADEMIC PROBATION

I was placed on academic probation
It's a severe notification

That if I didn't clean up my ways
I was entering my very last days

The reason for this trial
I had become a little wild

I had misguided my priority
Spent mornings playing Atari

I decided I had to leave it alone
Didn't want to get sent home

So happy that didn't turn out bad
And I can say I'm an FSU Grad.

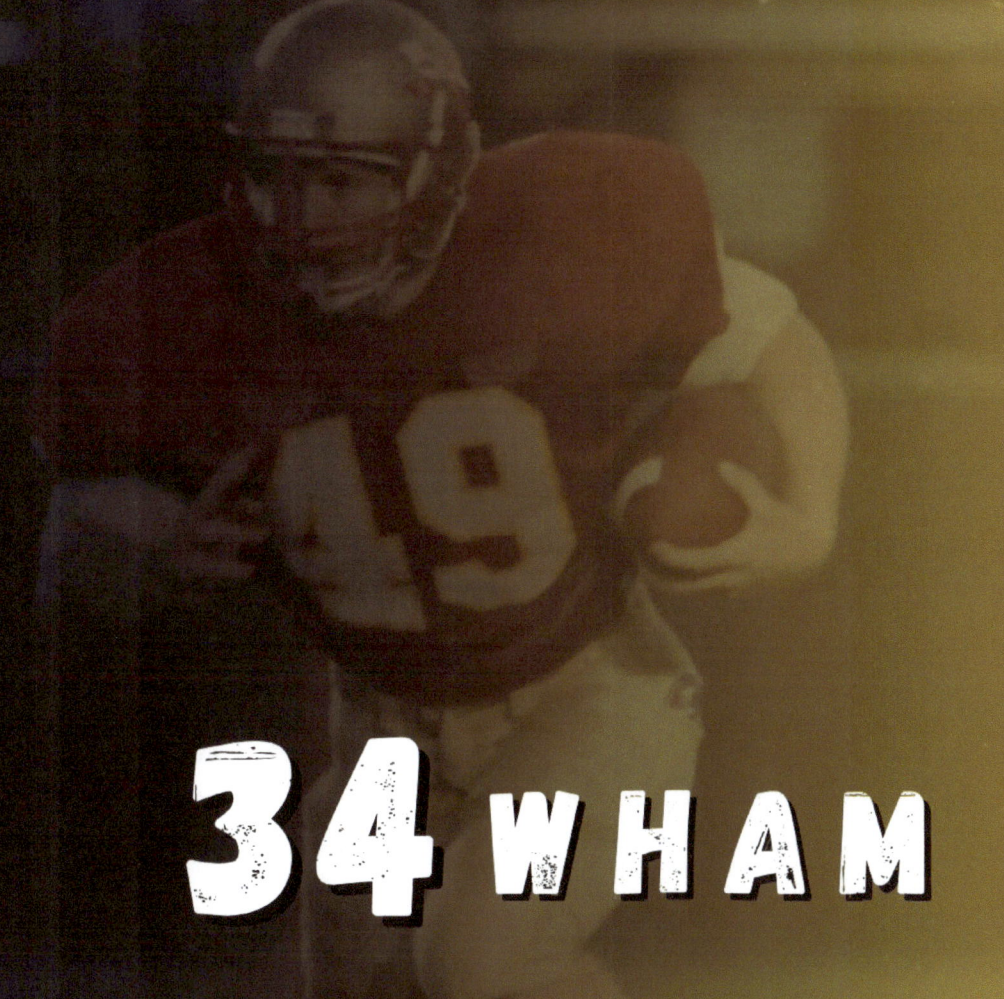

34 WHAM

Coach Bowden had a play called 34 WHAM
Dayne Williams scored TDs, a battering ram
It worked many times and got us out a Jam
Defense knew it was coming, McDuffie didn't give a damn
Pat Tomberlin, Tom O'Malley and me
The ball ran behind us three
Some defenses had better call the cops
Because that play was not gonna be stopped
The 3 of us and Dayne were gonna wreck shop
Which helped the Noles finish atop.

FAMU

MY PARENTS MET AT FAMU
MARRIAGE FAILED, BUT THAT BABY DUE
I WAS RAISED A RATTLER AT HEART
WANTED TO GO THERE PLAY AND START
I REMEMBER WHEN THEY WON IN '78
RUDY HUBBARD LED A TEAM THAT WAS GREAT
AT THE CLASSIC WHEN HELD IN TAMPA BAY
LOVED ALL THE BLACK FOLKS & THE MUSIC THEY'D PLAY
BUT THEY NEVER RECRUITED ME TO FAMU
SIGNED WITH STATE, KIN SAY, DAMN YOU
I DON'T REGRET MY CHOICE AT ALL
ALL I WANTED TO DO WAS PLAY BALL
MY MOM, SIS AND NEPHEW
ALL GRADUATED FROM FAMU
HAD PLENTY COUSINS, THAT ATTENDED MANY FALLS
ONE COUSIN IS EVEN IN THEIR HALL
ALL MY LIFE I'VE BEEN A BATTLER
SO PROUD OF ALL MY FAMU RATTLERS

ODELL HAGGINS

Odell was my next door neighbor
He didn't mind putting in that labor
Đell was a jokester coming in
Hard to be that, with a big head and chin
Moved from linebacker to nose
Which created problems for our foes
Had some really good times in school
Over the years we check in and still cool
He's been an assistant from Bobby
Bowden to Coach Norvell
Coaching Đ-Line is where he excelled
He's part of that class of 85
I must admit them boys was live
He's the essence of FSU Royalty
A player, a coach and also his loyalty
I'm so proud of my friend
Gotta get up there to see him again

KING OF THE BOARDS

Board Drills are 1 on 1, offense against D
There's always a defender, lined in front of me
Freshman year, new on the block
I was holding my own to everyone's shock
There was a change by year 2
Those defenders were beginning to get run thru
Year 3 brought a whole new thing
Couldn't be whipped, unofficially named King
But the coaches had to act a little fickle
Went and got DT Gerald Nichols
He was the real deal and he played hard
Too stumpy, couldn't get under that nose guard
That was fun taking that swing
Not my normal fighting ring
The coaches wanted to see our little fling
LBs and Ends knew what I bring
They couldn't deny #85 was King

MY MOTHER SAVED ME

FSU was in The Gator Bowl in 1985
Thank goodness my mother kept my
eligibility alive
She wanted to come to this game
And if she didn't, I'd have brought her
shame
This event Hassan Jones lost his
eligibility
Selling his tickets to our enemy
They turned him in to the NCAA
Then they announced he's ineligible to
play
Thank goodness she attended that game
Or my fate would have been the same
The people who did that was lame
God is Good I am gonna exclaim

ABOUT THE AUTHOR

Carter, from Sarasota, Florida, was a four-year letterman for the Seminoles during an important stretch in program history, from 1984-1987, a span of time leading up to and beginning the dynasty from '87-2001. And Carter, an outstanding blocker with reliable hands, was instrumental in improving the 'Noles from seven wins in his first season to an 11-1 record in his last. 1987 saw FSU finish second in the AP Poll, its highest final ranking in school history to that point.

Carter's individual accolades began in his junior season, when he was an honorable mention AP All-American in 1986. He followed that up by improving to a second-team AP selection in his senior year, when The Sporting News recognized him as a first-team All-American. Carter was a first team All-South Independent honoree in both '86 and '87. Until Nick O'Leary captured consensus All-America honors in 2014, Carter was the only Seminole TE ever to be named a second-team All-American.

A 44-game starter who was undefeated in four bowl games, Carter finished his FSU career with 71 catches for 777 yards and seven scores.

The Detroit Lions made Carter the first Seminole off the board in the 1988 NFL Draft when they chose him in the second round. He had a solid 10-year NFL career before serving as an assistant coach. In 2015, Carter was inducted into the Florida State Hall of Fame.

Coming Soon

WENDELL PATRICK CARTER

4 YEAR STARTER

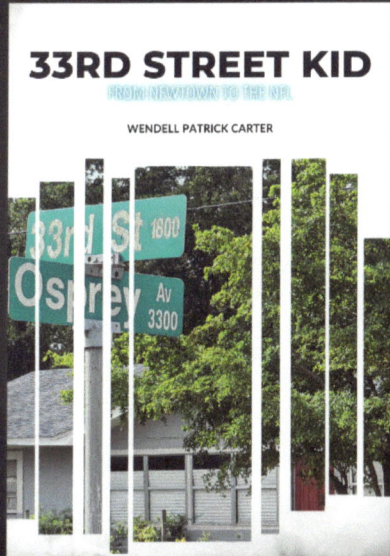

33RD STREET KID

FROM NEWTOWN TO THE NFL

WENDELL PATRICK CARTER

GUIDED BY GOD

Inspirational Poems by Wendell Patrick Carter

Got an idea for a book? Contact Curry Brothers Publishing, LLC. We are not satisfied until your publishing dreams come true. We specialize in all genres of books, especially religion, leadership, family history, poetry, and children's literature. There is an African Proverb that confirms, *"When an elder dies, a library closes."* Be careful who tells your family history. Ensure their values are your family's values? Our staff will navigate you through the entire publishing process and we take pride in going the extra mile in meeting your publishing goals. Improving the world one book at a time!

Curry Brothers Publishing, LLC
PO Box 247 Haymarket, VA 20168
Office: (888) 726-1824

Visit us at www.currybrotherspublishing.com

www.ingramcontent.com/pod-product-compliance
Lightning Source LLC
Chambersburg PA
CBHW040848120626
46547CB00001B/79